PLANES!
(and other things that fly)

THIS IS A WELBECK CHILDREN'S BOOK

Published in 2021 by Welbeck Children's Books
An imprint of Welbeck Children's Limited, part of Welbeck Publishing Group
20 Mortimer Street, London W1T 3JW

Associate Publisher: Laura Knowles
Commissioning Editor: Bryony Davies
Art Editor: Deborah Vickers
Design Manager: Emily Clarke
Designer: Melinda Penn
Production: Marion Storz

ISBN: 978-1-78312-650-7

Printed in Heshan, China

10 9 8 7 6 5 4 3 2 1

WELBECK

PLANES!

(and other things that fly)

Written by
Bryony Davies

Illustrated by
Maria Brzozowska

This book belongs to:

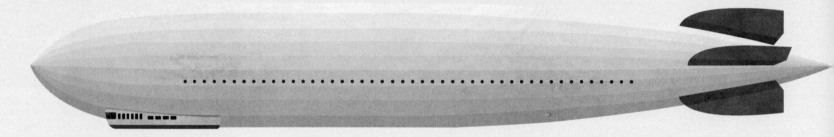

Contents

Amazing Airplanes 6

At the Air Show 8

How a Plane Flies 10

The First Flyers 12

Balloon Festival 14

Astonishing Aircraft 16

At the Airport 18

Inside an Airliner 20

Jobs to Do 22

Fly Your Own Plane 24

Military Aircraft 26

Flying Machine Challenge! 28

Helpful Helicopters 30

To the Rescue 32

Inside a Rescue Helicopter 34

Anything but Planes! 36

At the Gliding Club 38

Up into Space 40

Lift Off! 42

Fun Flying Facts 44

Can You Spot? 46

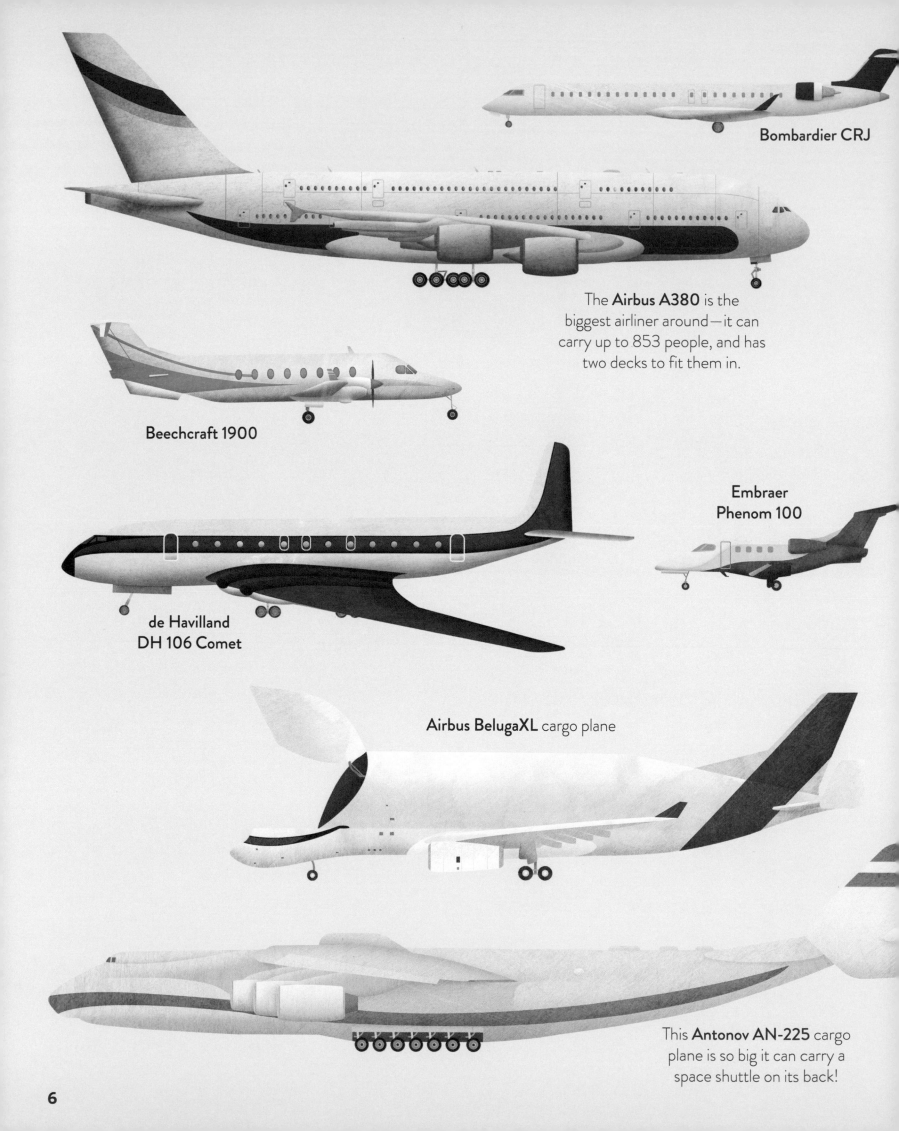

Bombardier CRJ

The **Airbus A380** is the biggest airliner around—it can carry up to 853 people, and has two decks to fit them in.

Beechcraft 1900

Embraer
Phenom 100

de Havilland
DH 106 Comet

Airbus **BelugaXL** cargo plane

This **Antonov AN-225** cargo plane is so big it can carry a space shuttle on its back!

Cessna SkyCourier
cargo plane

The **Airbus A320** is a bestselling airliner, and is flown by airlines across the world.

The **Douglas DC-2** was one of the first airliners, and it helped to make plane travel popular.

Amazing Airplanes

Airliners are planes that carry passengers. Some take hundreds of excited people on vacation. Others carry just a few people over much shorter distances. Cargo planes don't carry people, they carry things instead. They are designed with big doors to allow large loads on, and large spaces inside so they can carry a big load at a time.

Learjet

McDonnell Douglas DC-9

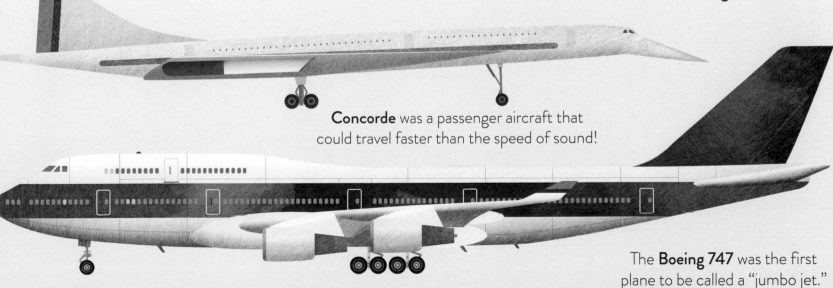

Concorde was a passenger aircraft that could travel faster than the speed of sound!

The **Boeing 747** was the first plane to be called a "jumbo jet."

Skywriting planes write words
and draw pictures in the sky.

Would you be brave
enough to walk on
the wing of a plane?

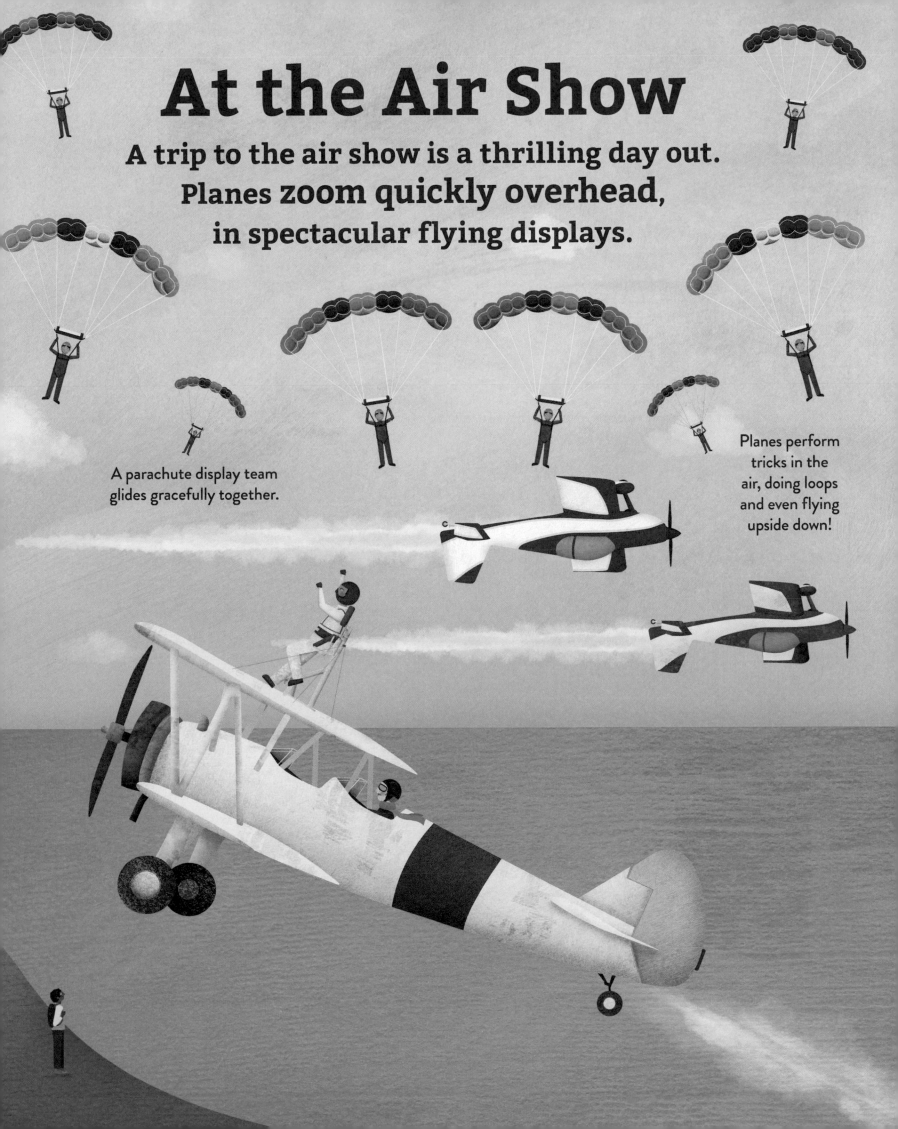

At the Air Show

A trip to the air show is a thrilling day out.
Planes **zoom** quickly overhead,
in spectacular flying displays.

A parachute display team
glides gracefully together.

Planes perform
tricks in the
air, doing loops
and even flying
upside down!

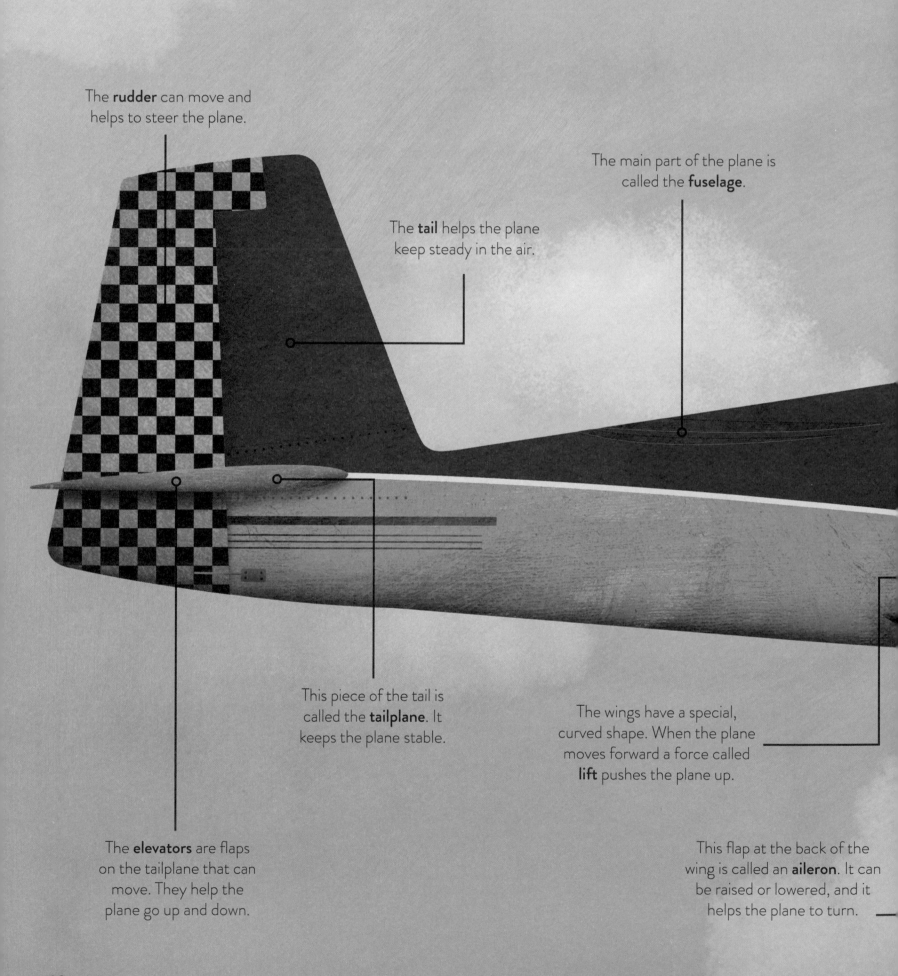

The **rudder** can move and helps to steer the plane.

The main part of the plane is called the **fuselage**.

The **tail** helps the plane keep steady in the air.

This piece of the tail is called the **tailplane**. It keeps the plane stable.

The wings have a special, curved shape. When the plane moves forward a force called **lift** pushes the plane up.

The **elevators** are flaps on the tailplane that can move. They help the plane go up and down.

This flap at the back of the wing is called an **aileron**. It can be raised or lowered, and it helps the plane to turn.

How a Plane Flies

Planes of all shapes and sizes can take off and fly high up in the sky. But how do they do it?

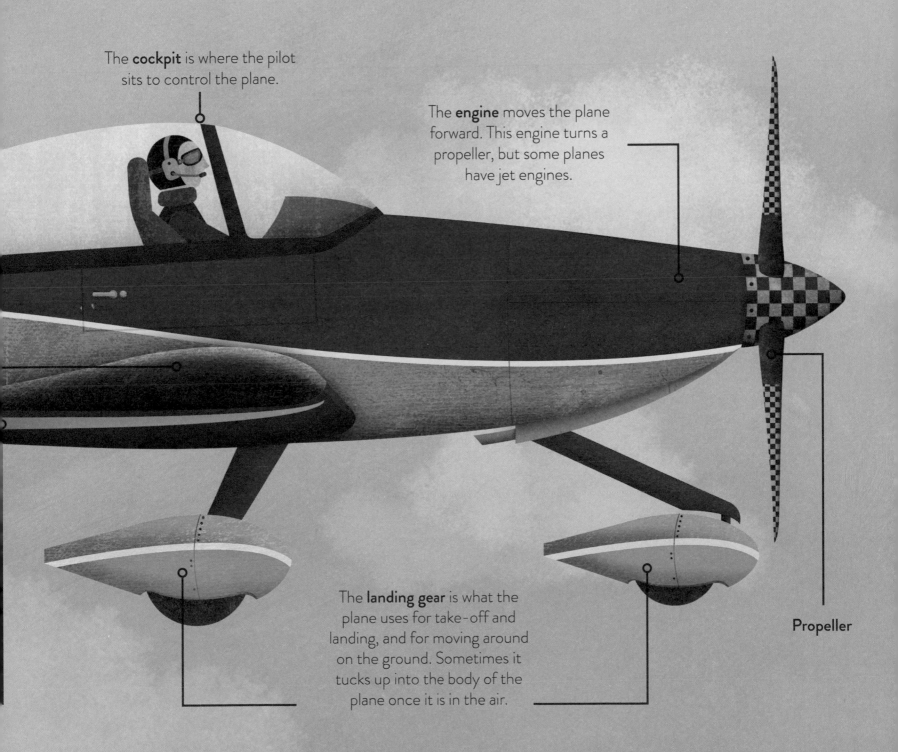

The **cockpit** is where the pilot sits to control the plane.

The **engine** moves the plane forward. This engine turns a propeller, but some planes have jet engines.

The **landing gear** is what the plane uses for take-off and landing, and for moving around on the ground. Sometimes it tucks up into the body of the plane once it is in the air.

Propeller

The **LZ 127** *Graf Zeppelin* could hold up to 20 passengers in the gondola (compartment) at the front.

The First Flyers

People first began to fly in hot-air balloons, floating up into the sky. Other inventors created gliders, which flew without engines. The first flight in a powered aircraft only lasted 12 seconds. That's not very long—but soon pilots were flying high in the sky for longer!

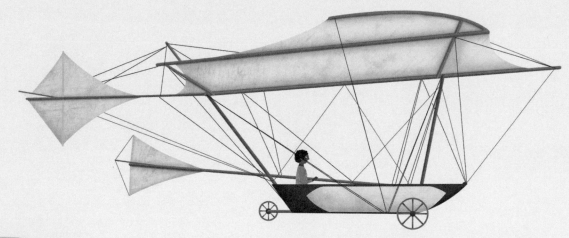

The **Cayley Glider** was the first glider to carry a person.

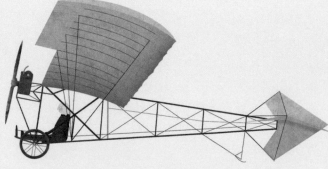

The engine and propeller of the **Santos-Dumont Demoiselle 20** were in front of the wings. *Demoiselle* is a French word meaning "dragonfly."

Avro Triplane IV

The *Steerable* **Balloon** had paddles on the basket that were designed to steer it.

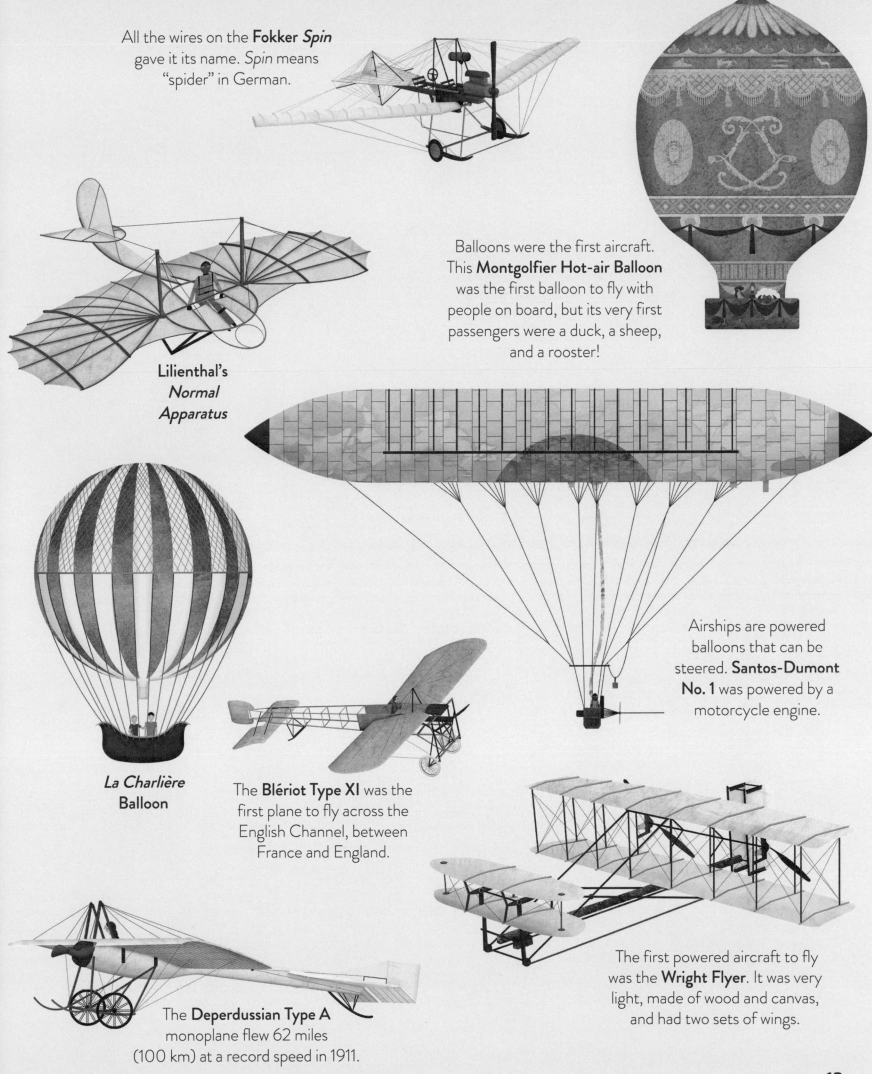

All the wires on the **Fokker *Spin*** gave it its name. *Spin* means "spider" in German.

Balloons were the first aircraft. This **Montgolfier Hot-air Balloon** was the first balloon to fly with people on board, but its very first passengers were a duck, a sheep, and a rooster!

Lilienthal's *Normal Apparatus*

Airships are powered balloons that can be steered. **Santos-Dumont No. 1** was powered by a motorcycle engine.

***La Charlière* Balloon**

The **Blériot Type XI** was the first plane to fly across the English Channel, between France and England.

The **Deperdussian Type A** monoplane flew 62 miles (100 km) at a record speed in 1911.

The first powered aircraft to fly was the **Wright Flyer**. It was very light, made of wood and canvas, and had two sets of wings.

Balloon Festival

The envelope is made of strong, light fabric.

The basket is attached to the envelope with strong cables. Balloon baskets can carry up to 24 people.

Hot-air balloons can sometimes land with a bump!

At the hot-air balloon festival, the sky is filled with brightly colored balloons. People ride in the baskets that hang below, floating up, up, and away.

Whoosh! The burners make a loud noise.

As the balloon fills with air it starts to take shape.

The burners set fire to the fuel. The fire warms the air inside the envelope, and the hot air inside the envelope makes it rise.

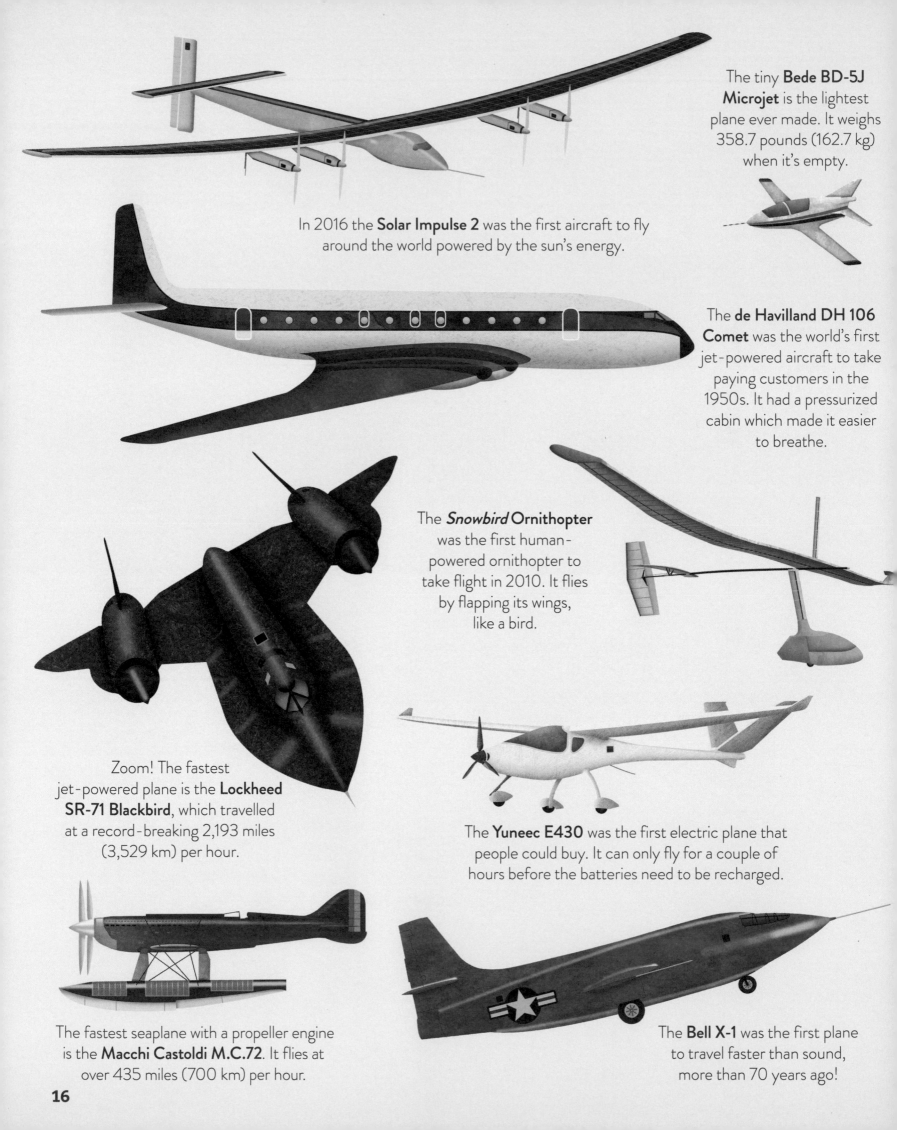

The tiny **Bede BD-5J Microjet** is the lightest plane ever made. It weighs 358.7 pounds (162.7 kg) when it's empty.

In 2016 the **Solar Impulse 2** was the first aircraft to fly around the world powered by the sun's energy.

The **de Havilland DH 106 Comet** was the world's first jet-powered aircraft to take paying customers in the 1950s. It had a pressurized cabin which made it easier to breathe.

The *Snowbird* Ornithopter was the first human-powered ornithopter to take flight in 2010. It flies by flapping its wings, like a bird.

Zoom! The fastest jet-powered plane is the **Lockheed SR-71 Blackbird**, which travelled at a record-breaking 2,193 miles (3,529 km) per hour.

The **Yuneec E430** was the first electric plane that people could buy. It can only fly for a couple of hours before the batteries need to be recharged.

The fastest seaplane with a propeller engine is the **Macchi Castoldi M.C.72**. It flies at over 435 miles (700 km) per hour.

The **Bell X-1** was the first plane to travel faster than sound, more than 70 years ago!

The first flight around the world was completed in 1924 by a **Douglas World Cruiser**.

A **Vickers Vimy** was the first plane to fly across the Atlantic Ocean without stopping, over a hundred years ago.

This **Supermarine S6B** seaplane was the fastest vehicle on Earth in 1931.

Astonishing Aircraft

These incredible aircraft broke records and did amazing things for the first time. Can you imagine being the first person to fly around the world?

The **Rutan Model 76 Voyager** was the first plane to fly around the world without refueling, 35 years ago. It took nine days.

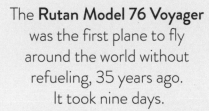

This **de Havilland DH.60G Gipsy Moth** is named *Jason I*. It belonged to a pilot called Amy Johnson. She was the first person to fly on her own from Great Britain to Australia in 1930. That's a long way!

In 1927 a pilot named Charles Lindbergh flew the **Ryan NYP** *Spirit of St Louis* on his own, non-stop from New York to Paris. It took him 33 ½ hours!

At the Airport

A busy airport can have hundreds of thousands of people passing through every day, traveling to and from places all around the world.

Control tower

When a plane drives along a runway we say it "taxis."

At busy airports, planes will take off and land quickly, one after another. Planes that are waiting to land circle in the air above the airport until it's their turn.

The terminal is where people check in and drop off their luggage before getting on their plane.

When the plane is going fast enough, the pilot lifts the nose and it takes off, into the air.

Runway

Inside an Airliner

Huge airliners are like busy cities in the sky. They carry hundreds of passengers vast distances across the world. Take a peek to find out what goes on inside.

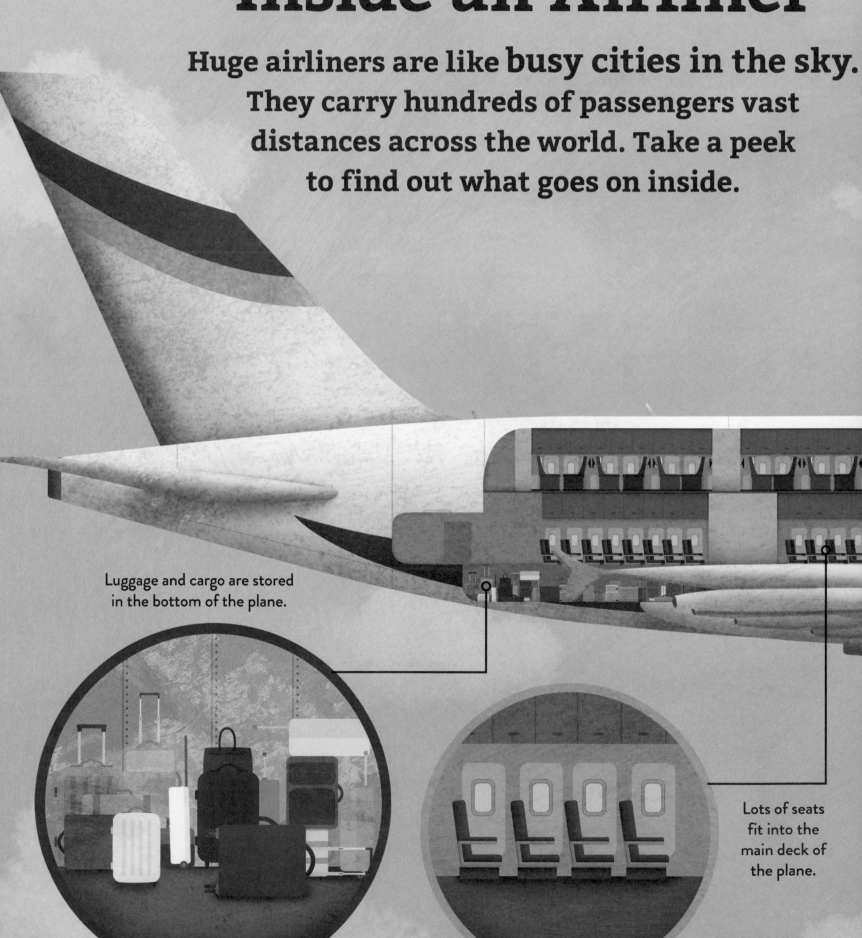

Luggage and cargo are stored in the bottom of the plane.

Lots of seats fit into the main deck of the plane.

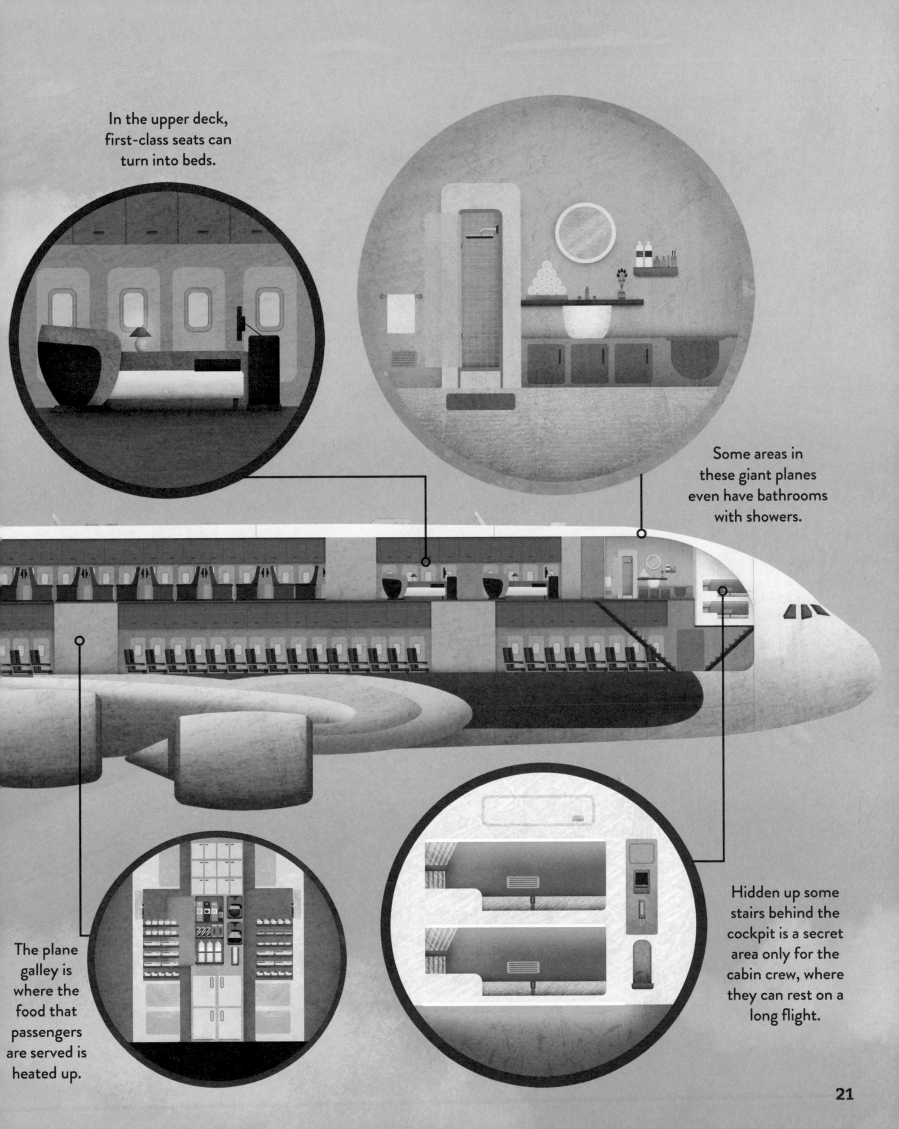

In the upper deck, first-class seats can turn into beds.

Some areas in these giant planes even have bathrooms with showers.

The plane galley is where the food that passengers are served is heated up.

Hidden up some stairs behind the cockpit is a secret area only for the cabin crew, where they can rest on a long flight.

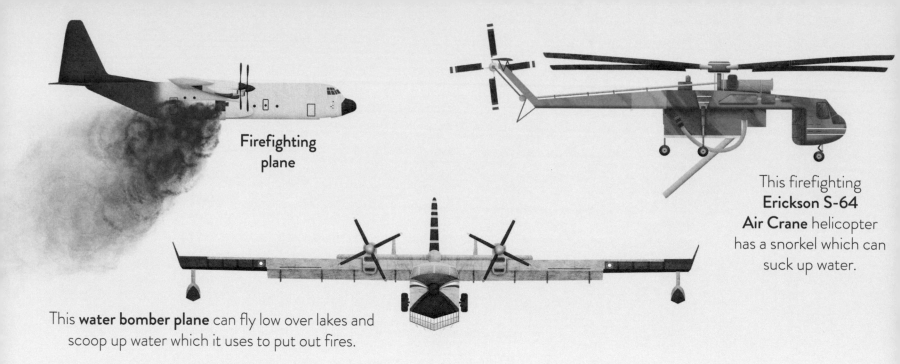

Firefighting plane

This firefighting **Erickson S-64 Air Crane** helicopter has a snorkel which can suck up water.

This **water bomber plane** can fly low over lakes and scoop up water which it uses to put out fires.

Jobs to Do

Planes and helicopters can be helping hands in the air.
They can fly in to fight a fire or rescue an injured person.
They are flying hospitals and can even chase storms
to find out more about them.

The **Royal Flying Doctor Service** flies to people in trouble in Australia, which is such a big country that it would take too long to get to many places by road.

This plane takes firefighters called **smoke jumpers** to the scenes of fires. They parachute out so they can fight the fire.

Ski plane

This **hurricane hunter** follows storms so that scientists can learn about weather.

Police helicopter

Search and rescue helicopter

Cropdusters spray seeds or fertilizer onto farmers' fields.

Bush planes are tough planes with big wheels to help them land on rough ground in remote places.

Skywriter

Heli-loggers can carry heavy trees when they've been cut down.

This **wildlife trooper helicopter** helps people look after wildlife. It can land on water and land.

Aerobatic plane

This **herding helicopter** guides horses and other animals on ranches.

Air ambulance

Fly Your Own Plane

The **head-up display** is a seethrough display that lets the pilot see important information at the same time as they look through the windshield.

A1

The pilot usually sits in the left-hand seat.

Rudder pedals steer the plane.

Military Aircraft

Aircraft are used by armies around the world, and they can do some pretty amazing things. Some are small and fast, and others are used to carry people and heavy machinery. Some of these aircraft aren't used any more, but they are very famous.

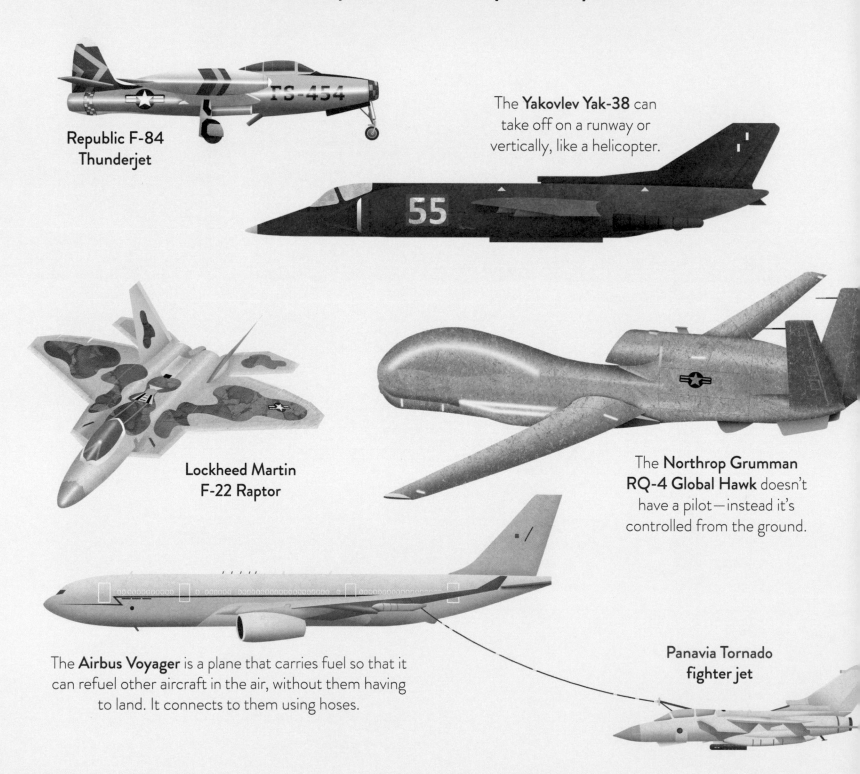

Republic F-84 Thunderjet

The **Yakovlev Yak-38** can take off on a runway or vertically, like a helicopter.

Lockheed Martin F-22 Raptor

The **Northrop Grumman RQ-4 Global Hawk** doesn't have a pilot—instead it's controlled from the ground.

The **Airbus Voyager** is a plane that carries fuel so that it can refuel other aircraft in the air, without them having to land. It connects to them using hoses.

Panavia Tornado fighter jet

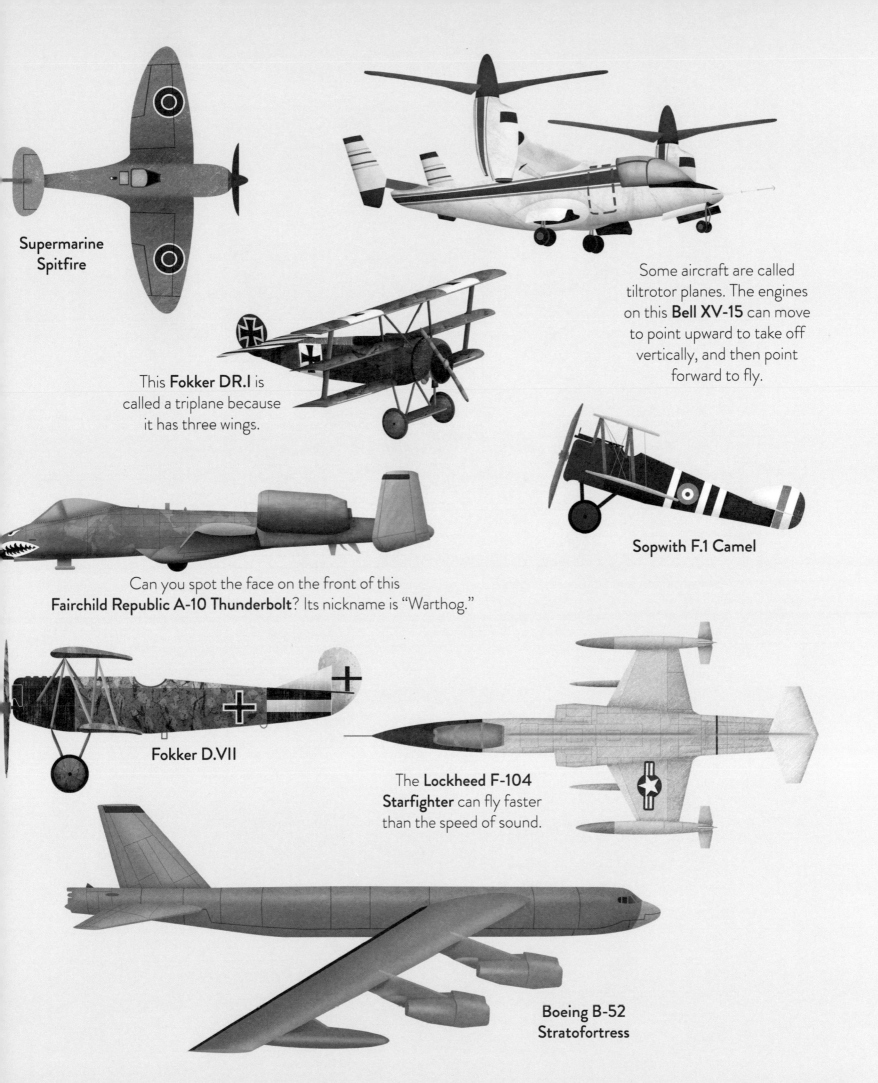

Supermarine
Spitfire

Some aircraft are called
tiltrotor planes. The engines
on this **Bell XV-15** can move
to point upward to take off
vertically, and then point
forward to fly.

This **Fokker DR.I** is
called a triplane because
it has three wings.

Sopwith F.1 Camel

Can you spot the face on the front of this
Fairchild Republic A-10 Thunderbolt? Its nickname is "Warthog."

Fokker D.VII

The **Lockheed F-104
Starfighter** can fly faster
than the speed of sound.

Boeing B-52
Stratofortress

Flying Machine Challenge!

It's competition time! Teams from far and wide have brought their wild and wacky flying machines to the Flying Machine Challenge, and now it's time to see which one will fly the farthest.

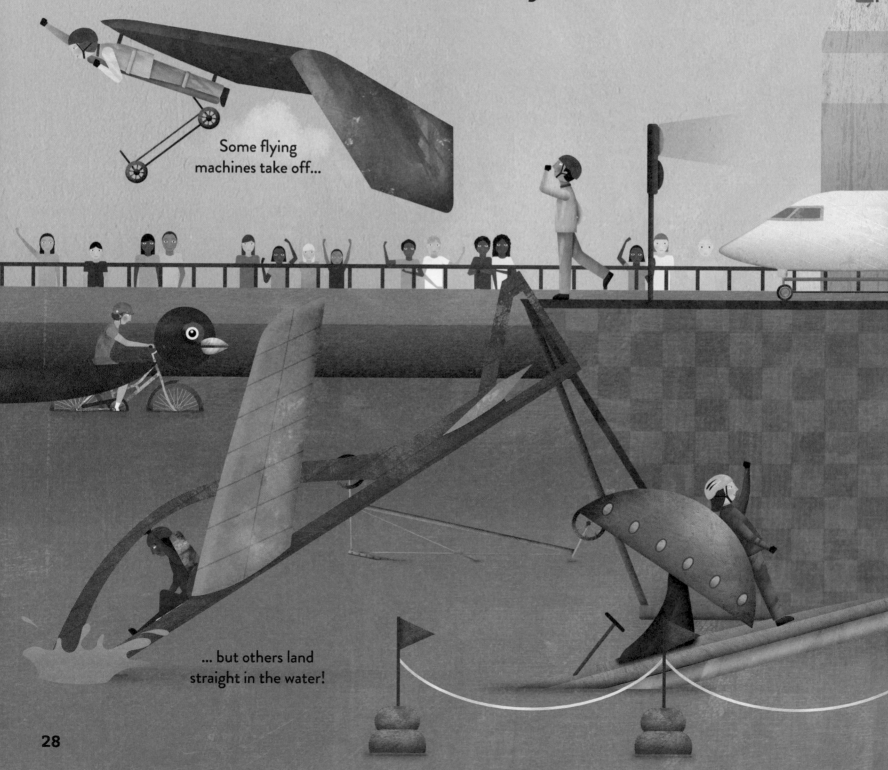

Some flying machines take off...

... but others land straight in the water!

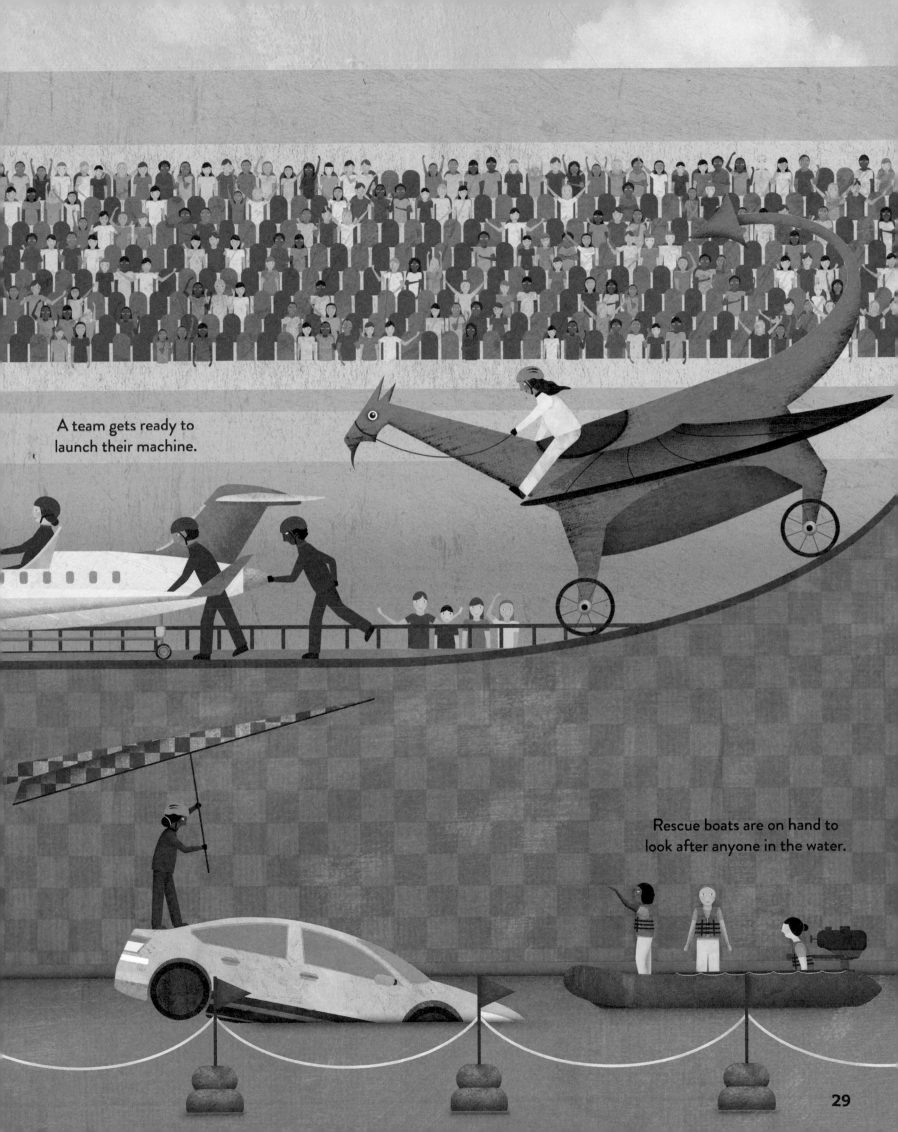

A team gets ready to launch their machine.

Rescue boats are on hand to look after anyone in the water.

29

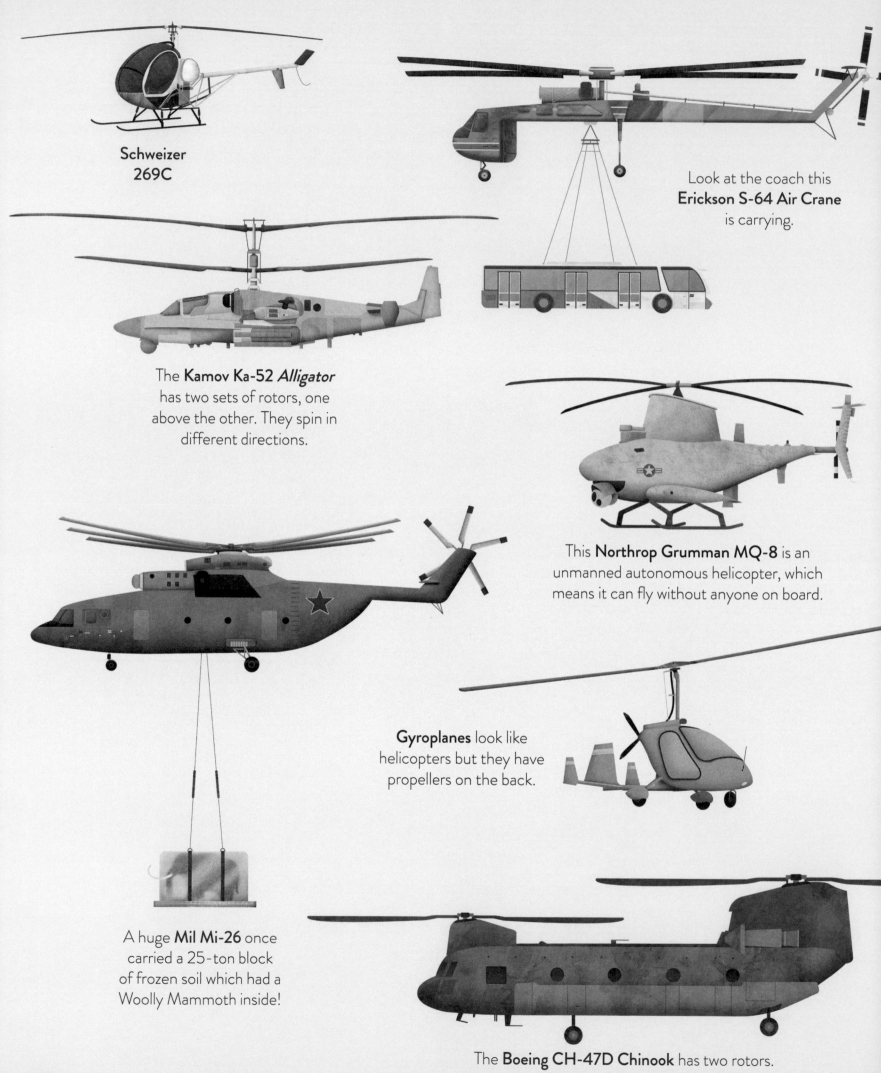

Schweizer
269C

Look at the coach this
Erickson S-64 Air Crane
is carrying.

The **Kamov Ka-52** *Alligator*
has two sets of rotors, one
above the other. They spin in
different directions.

This **Northrop Grumman MQ-8** is an
unmanned autonomous helicopter, which
means it can fly without anyone on board.

Gyroplanes look like
helicopters but they have
propellers on the back.

A huge **Mil Mi-26** once
carried a 25-ton block
of frozen soil which had a
Woolly Mammoth inside!

The **Boeing CH-47D Chinook** has two rotors.

Wallis WA-116

This **Westland Dragonfly HR3** has folding rotor blades so it can be stored on a ship.

Airbus H135

The **Eurocopter X³** is a bit like a helicopter and a bit like a plane. It has a rotor on top, but it also has two extra propellers.

Bell 206 Jetranger

Helpful Helicopters

What's that hovering in the air? It's a helicopter!
The parts that spin around are called 'rotor blades'.
They move so quickly that they become a blur.

AgustaWestland Apache
AH Mk 1 attack helicopter

The **Bell 47** has two blades on its rotor.

To the Rescue

There's been an accident high up in the mountains, but here's a rescue helicopter, **coming to save the day!** Rotors whir as it hovers above, ready to take an injured person to safety.

A mountain rescue vehicle waits nearby.

The helicopter doesn't land on the mountainside. Instead it stays in the air, and uses its winch to lower down rescuers.

A stretcher is lowered down, and the injured person is loaded on. Then they are carefully winched back up.

A hatch at the back opens so that the stretcher can be wheeled out of the helicopter once it has landed.

Inside a Rescue Helicopter

Rescue helicopters can respond to emergencies really quickly, flying straight to the scene.

There's a stretcher inside the helicopter for patients who need to lie down.

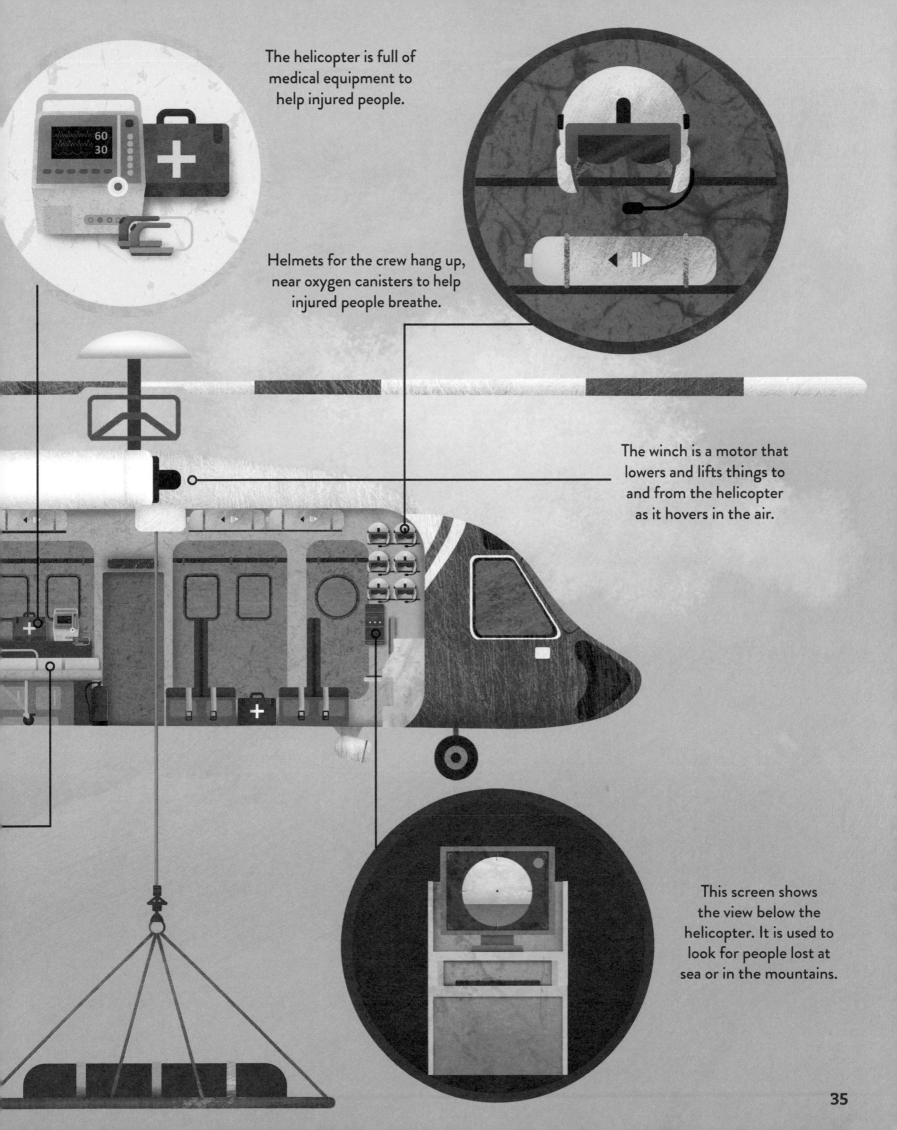

The helicopter is full of medical equipment to help injured people.

Helmets for the crew hang up, near oxygen canisters to help injured people breathe.

The winch is a motor that lowers and lifts things to and from the helicopter as it hovers in the air.

This screen shows the view below the helicopter. It is used to look for people lost at sea or in the mountains.

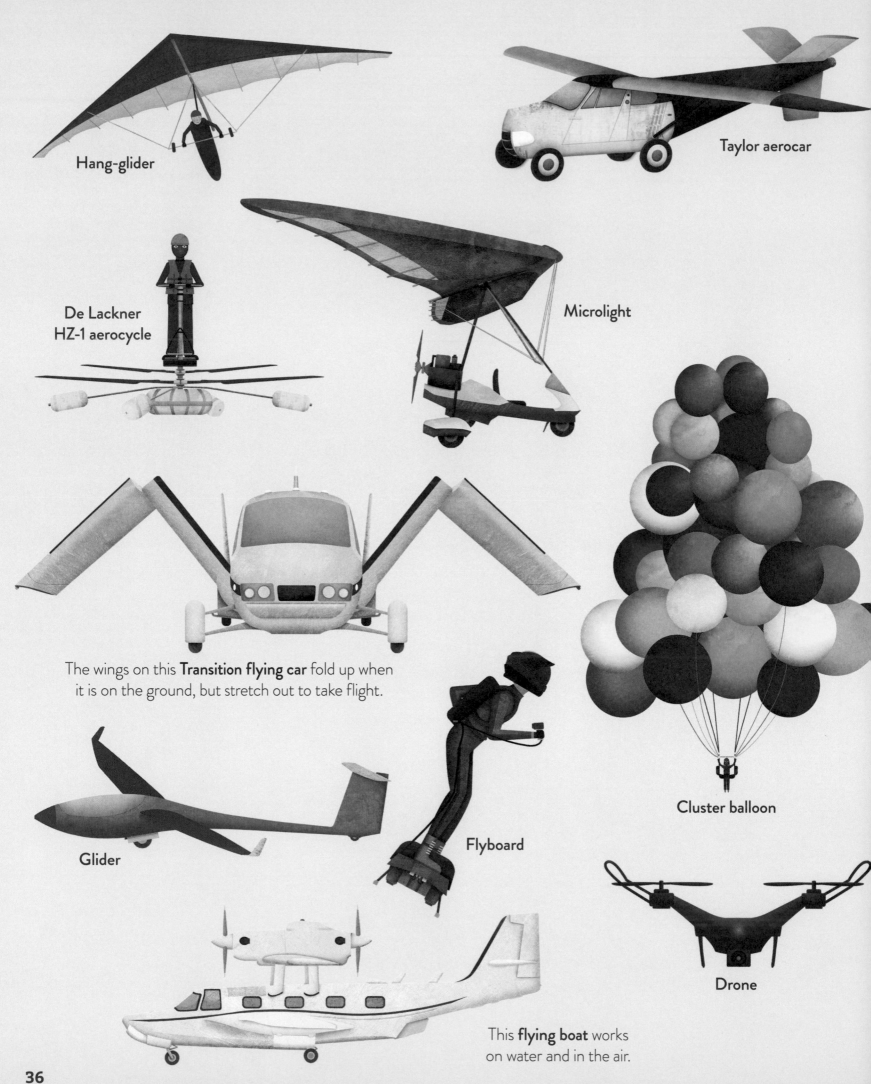

Hang-glider

Taylor aerocar

De Lackner HZ-1 aerocycle

Microlight

The wings on this **Transition flying car** fold up when it is on the ground, but stretch out to take flight.

Cluster balloon

Glider

Flyboard

Drone

This **flying boat** works on water and in the air.

Anything but Planes!

It's not just planes and helicopters that can fly high in the sky.
You can also take off in a hang-glider or a hot-air balloon.
Or have you ever thought of driving a flying car,
or wearing a jet-powered wingsuit?

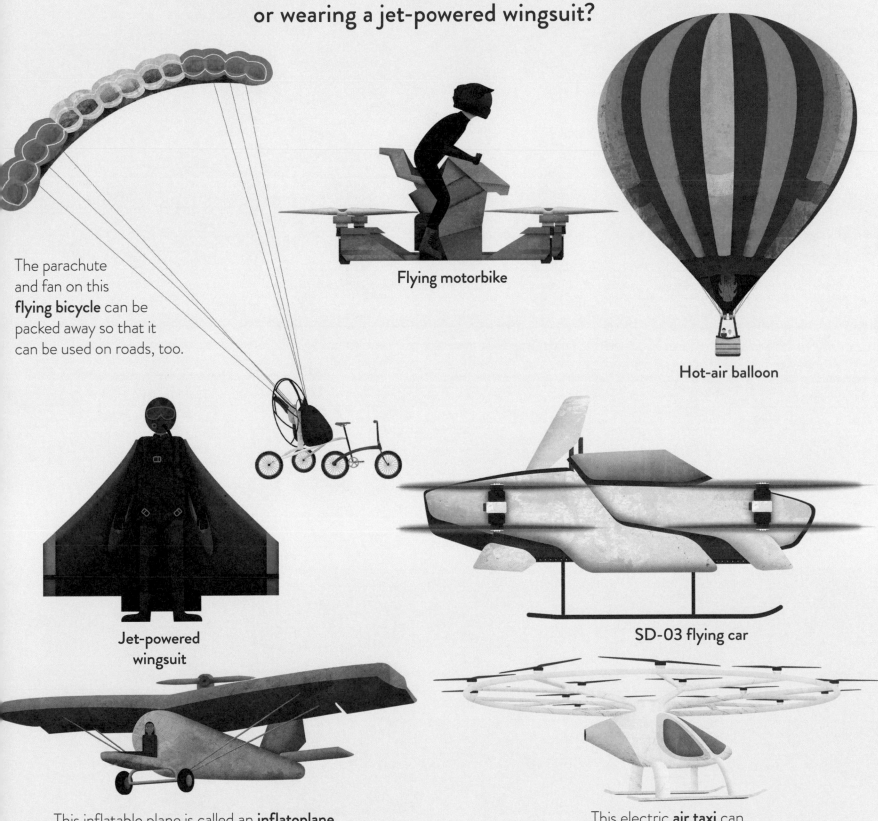

The parachute and fan on this **flying bicycle** can be packed away so that it can be used on roads, too.

Flying motorbike

Hot-air balloon

Jet-powered wingsuit

SD-03 flying car

This inflatable plane is called an **inflatoplane**, but not many were made because it could be popped!

This electric **air taxi** can carry two people.

At the Gliding Club

Gliders line up, ready for take-off.

Small planes can tow gliders up into the air so they take flight.

Gliders swoop quietly through the air because they don't have engines. They use rising air to keep them flying —but they can stay up in the air for hours and hours!

Gliders are kept in tip-top condition in the workshop.

Winches can launch gliders up into the air at top speed, then they glide around gracefully in the sky.

39

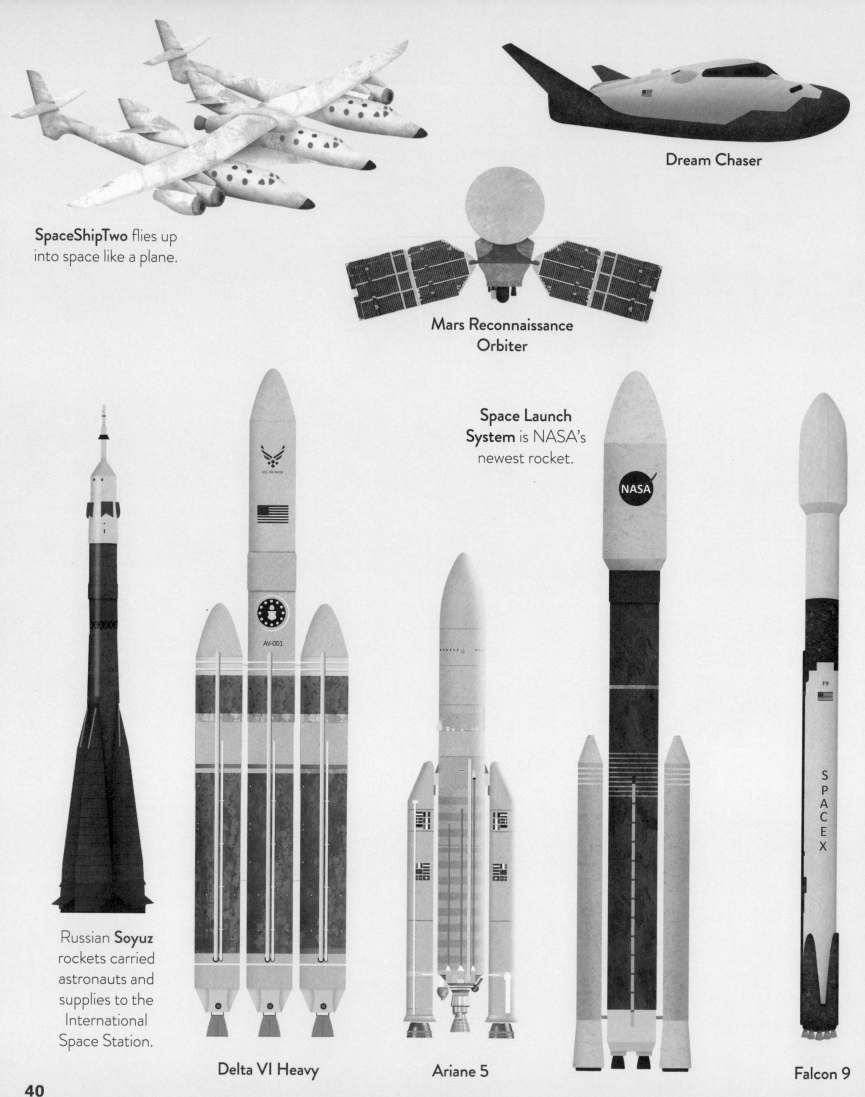

SpaceShipTwo flies up into space like a plane.

Dream Chaser

Mars Reconnaissance Orbiter

Space Launch System is NASA's newest rocket.

Russian **Soyuz** rockets carried astronauts and supplies to the International Space Station.

Delta VI Heavy

Ariane 5

Falcon 9

Up into Space

Huge, rocket-powered launch vehicles blast up from the ground, carrying spacecraft and satellites up, up, and away, far into space!

Space Shuttle

UNITED STATES

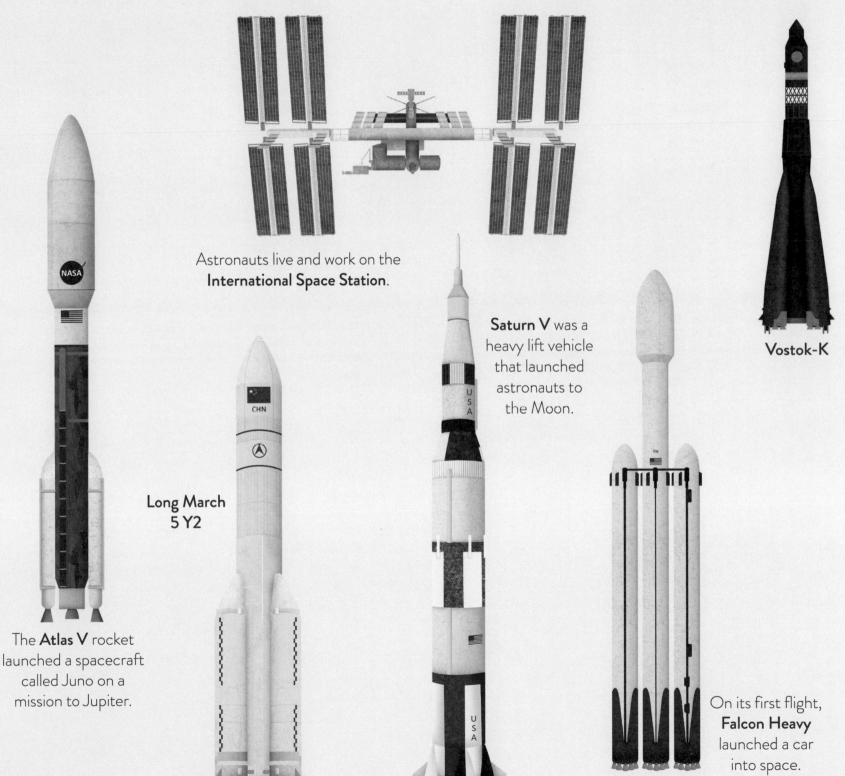

Astronauts live and work on the **International Space Station**.

Vostok-K

The **Atlas V** rocket launched a spacecraft called Juno on a mission to Jupiter.

Long March 5 Y2

Saturn V was a heavy lift vehicle that launched astronauts to the Moon.

On its first flight, **Falcon Heavy** launched a car into space.

Liftoff!

It's time for lift-off at the space center. The space shuttle is about to launch into space.

Launch tower

Astronauts walked across this access arm, 148 feet (45 m) up in the air, toward the shuttle.

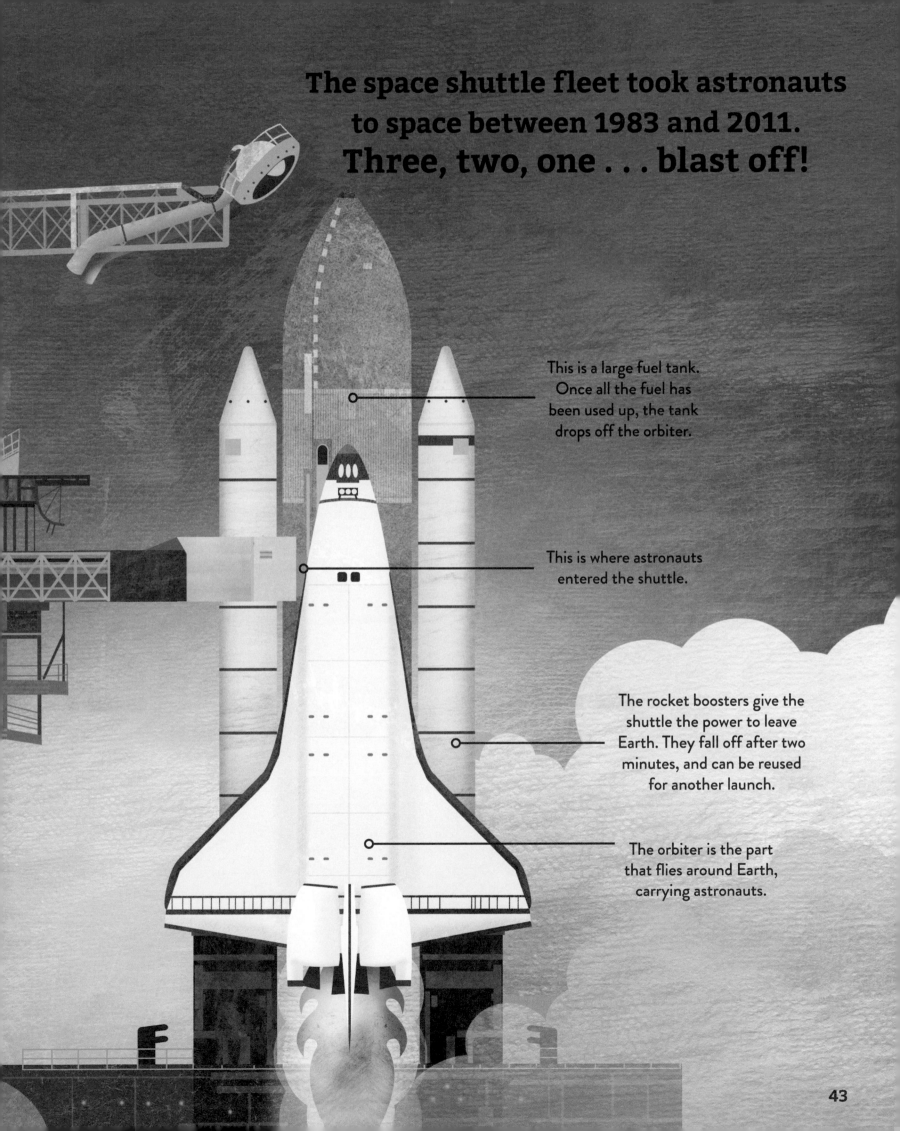

The space shuttle fleet took astronauts to space between 1983 and 2011. Three, two, one . . . blast off!

This is a large fuel tank. Once all the fuel has been used up, the tank drops off the orbiter.

This is where astronauts entered the shuttle.

The rocket boosters give the shuttle the power to leave Earth. They fall off after two minutes, and can be reused for another launch.

The orbiter is the part that flies around Earth, carrying astronauts.

Fun Flying Facts

1. Each engine on an Airbus A380 weighs almost 13,890 pounds (6,300 kg). That's the same amount as a big male elephant.

2. One old Boeing 727 has been turned into a room in a hotel in Costa Rica. It is high up in the trees in the jungle.

3. Unlike planes, helicopters can fly forward, backward, and sideways.

4. Have you ever wondered why plane windows have rounded corners, not square ones? This makes them stronger so they don't break when the air pressure in the plane changes as it flies.

5. When you fly, your taste buds—which help you taste your food—don't work so well. That's why if you've ever been on a flight, your snack might not have been as tasty as it usually is!

6. Air Traffic Control towers make sure all the planes taking off and landing at an airport are in the right place. The tallest Air Traffic Control tower in the world is in Malaysia, at the Kuala Lumpur International Airport. It's 440 feet (134 m) tall, which is as tall as about 24 giraffes!

7. The air in a hot-air balloon is hotter than boiling water. That's hot!

8. Laika the dog was the first animal to orbit the Earth in a spaceship.

9. The Moon is the only place in space that humans have landed. They travelled there on a rocket called Saturn V.

10. A helicopter landed on the peak of Mount Everest, the world's highest mountain, in 2005.

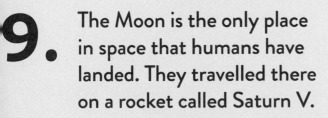

Can You Spot?

Take a look through the book and see which of these things you can find!

Bed

Balloon shaped like a mushroom

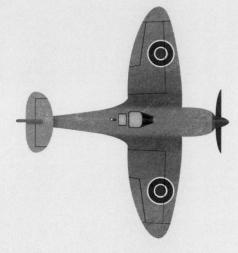

Supermarine Spitfire

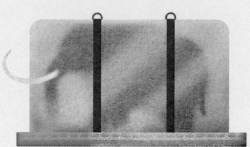

Woolly mammoth

Police helicopter

First aid kit

Winch

Skiers

Learjet

Parachutist

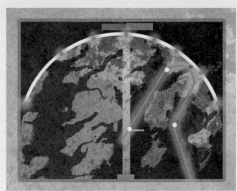

Navigation display

Vostok-K

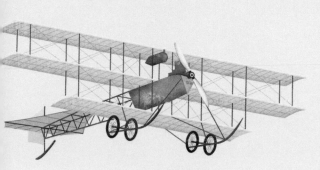

Avro Triplane IV

Bede BD-5J Microjet

Planes flying in formation

Picnic

Mountain chalet

Rescue helicopter screen

Four-wheel drive

Gyroplane

Two horses

Up,
up, and
away!